# Can't I Just

# Stop Feeling So

# Alone?

Jennifer Larsen

This book is a work of nonfiction intended to provide general guidance. It is not a substitute for professional advice. The author has made every effort to ensure the accuracy and completeness of the information contained herein, but assumes no responsibility for errors, omissions, or differing interpretations.

Originality Statement

This book is an original work written by the author and reflects their unique ideas, voice, and instructional approach. While it may reference common educational and career-planning concepts, all content, including structure, language, exercises, and framework, is the author's own creation. Any similarities to other published works are purely coincidental.

Printed in the United States of America

ISBN: 978-1-968756-84-0

First Edition

Cover design by Rachel Bostwick

Interior design and layout by Rachel Bostwick

For information or bulk orders, visit cantijust.com

## How to Use This Book

This book is two books in one.

You're starting with *Can't I Just Stop Feeling So Alone?*, which means you may be feeling isolated, tired of trying, or unsure how to connect. You are not alone in feeling this way – even if it's been a long time since anyone really said that to you.

This half of the book is here to validate what you're feeling and help you move through it at your own pace. No pressure.

When you feel ready – whether that's tomorrow, next month, or never – you can flip the book over and keep going.

Start where you are. That's enough.

# Contents

# ✳ Introduction

**You're not weak. You're not broken. You're just lonely. And that's a very real kind of pain.**

There's a kind of loneliness no one prepares you for.

It doesn't always come from being by yourself. It comes from *not being seen*.

It's being surrounded by classmates or coworkers and still feeling like you don't belong.

It's knowing people who'd say they care – but not knowing who you could actually call if something really went wrong.

It's the weight of every unanswered message, every birthday no one remembered, every laugh you weren't part of.

And maybe worst of all? It's the feeling that this might just be... *you now*. Like something shifted, and now you're the background character in everyone else's story. Not by choice. Just... faded out.

This book isn't going to guilt you into "getting out there."

It won't ask you to fake a smile or force connections that don't feel real.

And it definitely won't pretend that just "thinking positive" is enough to change everything.

Instead, this book is going to do what people should have done all along:

Sit with you. Listen. Help you figure out what this feeling is, where it came from, and – if you're ready – how to move through it without pretending you're fine.

We'll talk about why loneliness feels the way it does.

We'll look at the stories you might be telling yourself – the ones that whisper "you don't matter."

And we'll begin to gently untangle those lies from the truth.

You don't have to flip the book over yet. That part – the one about friendship and connection and how to try again – is still there, waiting.

Right now, you're here. And I'm here with you.

That's enough.

# Chapter 1:
# What Is Loneliness, Really?

Let's name it properly:

**Loneliness is not weakness. It's not failure. It's not you being broken.**

It's a signal – a very human signal – that your need for connection isn't being met.

Think of it like hunger. When your body is missing something vital, it tells you.

Loneliness is that same kind of alarm – but instead of food, it's *belonging* that's missing.


And here's the cruel part: once the loneliness alarm goes off, it actually gets *harder* to reach out.

You might second-guess everything you say. Worry that you're being too needy or too quiet or too much.

You start to assume people won't care – or worse, that they'll be annoyed by you.

So you back off. Stay quiet. Try not to bother anyone.


And then the loneliness grows.


That's not you being dramatic. That's your brain trying to protect you – from rejection, from disappointment, from being hurt again.

Unfortunately, it also protects you from connection. And that's where things start to spiral.

There are **different kinds of loneliness**, and you might feel more than one at a time:

- **Social loneliness:** You don't feel like you have a group or tribe you fit into.

- **Emotional loneliness:** You don't have anyone to open up to on a deeper level.

- **Situational loneliness:** You moved, changed schools, lost someone, or went through something that pulled you out of your circle.

- **Chronic loneliness:** The kind that's lasted for months or even years, and now feels like part of your personality.

- **Existential loneliness:** A heavy, quiet emptiness – where even when things look fine on the outside, you feel like something huge is missing.

Any one of those can leave you feeling disconnected, tired, unmotivated, or like you've lost something essential – but can't quite name what.

And most people? They don't see it.

They assume you're "doing fine" because you smile when you're supposed to. You show up. You nod.

But under the surface, it's lonely as hell.

Here's what I want you to know:

1.  You're not the only one feeling this.
2.  You're not wrong for feeling it.
3.  You don't have to stay here forever.

Loneliness is not a flaw in you.

It's a side effect of being alive in a world that doesn't always make space for quiet people, different people, grieving people, or those who don't know how to jump into conversations and friend groups like it's easy.

If no one's ever explained that to you before – let this be the first time someone does.

You're not weak.

You're not too late.

You're not invisible.

You're just lonely.

And that can change.

## Chapter 2:
## Why Am I Like This?
*(Spoiler: You're not "like this." You're reacting to life the best way you know how.)*

Let's start with the question you might not have said out loud – but I bet it's been circling in your head:

"Why am I like this? Why can't I connect like everyone else seems to?"

First of all: pause.

You don't owe the world a performance of "normal."

And the idea that "everyone else is fine" is a lie social media and hallway glances are really good at selling.

That kid who always has someone to talk to between classes? Might be terrified of being alone.

The one posting selfies with their "besties"? Might be crying themselves to sleep at night.

The loudest person in the room? Might be fighting off their own fear of being forgotten.

Just because they look connected doesn't mean they *feel* connected.

But okay, real talk. Let's say you *do* feel different. Like there's something about you that makes this harder.

**Here are some reasons you might be feeling this way – and none of them are your fault:**

**1. You moved, changed schools, or lost your social group.**

Major life transitions are lonely – even the good ones.

If your circle got disrupted, it's natural to feel adrift. Connection takes time to rebuild.

**2. You're shy, quiet, or socially anxious.**

Some people recharge alone. Others freeze in new situations.

None of that means you're incapable of friendship – it just means your social battery is different.

**3. You're neurodivergent.**

If you're autistic, ADHD, or otherwise wired differently, you may struggle with things like eye contact, social timing, or reading cues.

This doesn't mean you can't connect – it just means you weren't taught in a way that worked for *you.*

## 4. You've been hurt before.

Rejection. Betrayal. Abandonment.

When friendship has ended in pain, your brain learns to associate people with risk. So it pulls back. It walls off.

That's protection – not weakness.

## 5. You've built armor.

Maybe you joke too much so no one gets too close.

Maybe you ghost people before they can ghost you.

Maybe you pretend not to care because caring got you hurt.

Guess what? That's still human. You didn't mess up – you just adapted.

## 6. You live in a distracted world.

And then there's the part no one talks about enough:

People don't look up anymore.

You could be standing right next to someone, hoping for eye contact, a smile, *something* – but their face is buried in their phone. They're watching something. Texting someone. Checking nothing.

It's not that you're uninteresting. It's that the world has gotten noisy.

Loneliness today doesn't just come from being left out – it comes from being surrounded by people who *don't even notice you're there.*

That hurts. It's confusing. And it's not your fault.

**You're not "like this" because you're broken.**

You're like this because your experiences *shaped* you.

If no one modeled closeness or trust, how would you know how to build it?

If people dismissed your feelings, how would you know it's safe to express them?

If you were left out over and over again, of course you'd start to assume you're not wanted.

Loneliness often grows in the gap between what we *need* and what we *believe we deserve.*

And if you've been lonely for a while, you might have started believing that maybe this is just who you are now.

But that's the thing about loneliness: it doesn't show up because something's wrong with *you.*

It shows up because something's *missing.*

And missing things – connection, trust, warmth, shared laughter – that doesn't make you broken.

It makes you human.

So let's stop asking "what's wrong with me?"

And start asking: *What happened that made this feel so hard?*

Because that's a question with answers. And answers lead to healing.

# Chapter 3:
## The Stories We Tell Ourselves
*(And why they feel true – even when they're not.)*

Loneliness doesn't just sit quietly in the background.

It talks to you. It whispers things. It tells you stories.

And the worst part? Those stories start to sound like facts.

"No one really likes me."

"I'm not interesting."

"I'm always the one who has to try."

"They wouldn't notice if I disappeared."

"Everyone already has their group. There's no room for me."

"I'm too awkward. Too quiet. Too much. Too late."

Over time, these thoughts don't feel like thoughts anymore.

They feel like *truth.*

They slide into your self-talk, your inner voice, your expectations of the world.

They become the background music of your day:

Soft. Constant. Familiar. Wrong.

## 🧠 Where do these stories come from?

They come from moments that left a mark.

The time you weren't invited.

The friend who slowly drifted away.

The laugh someone gave when you finally tried to open up.

Loneliness doesn't just appear – it builds.

One missed text, one ignored wave, one uncomfortable lunch period at a time.

Eventually, your brain stops thinking *that hurt* and starts thinking *I must not matter.*

But here's the thing: our brains are designed to make sense of pain.

They'd rather come up with a bad story than have no story at all.

And if that story is *"I'm unlovable,"* it might hurt less than *"I don't know why this keeps happening."*

At least then you have an answer.

But it's the wrong one.

## 🕯 Mini Stories We Swallow Too Easily:

### 🪁 The Rejection Story:

"I tried once, and it didn't work. People must just not like me."

Truth: That one person wasn't your forever friend. That doesn't mean no one will be.

### 👻 The Ghosting Story:

"They stopped talking to me – so I must have done something wrong."

Truth: People leave for all kinds of reasons that have nothing to do with you.

Silence isn't always about blame. It's just silence.

**The Comparison Story:**

"Everyone else already has people. I missed my window."

Truth: There is no window. Friendships form at 12, 16, 25, 47, 88. Connection isn't a race. You're still in it.

**The Masking Story:**

"If I let people see the real me, they'll leave. I have to act a certain way to be liked."

Truth: The more you hide, the more alone you feel – even when you're technically "with" people.

Real closeness requires realness. Start small, but start true.

## 🧠 Try This Exercise: Rewrite the Narrative

Step 1: Write down a thought you've had recently that hurt.

Example: *"People always leave me."*

Step 2: Ask yourself:

- Is this **always** true?
- Has it been true for everyone I've ever met?
- Could there be **another explanation**?

Step 3: Reframe the story. Try for honesty + hope, not fake positivity.

→ New version:

*"Some people left. Others haven't shown up yet. But that doesn't mean no one will."*

## 🌿 You are not your worst-case scenario.

That voice in your head that says you're too much, too late, or too invisible?

That voice was built out of survival.

You believed those stories because they made rejection hurt a little less.

But now they're doing the opposite.

They're keeping you lonely – not safe.

You don't have to be cruel to yourself to protect yourself.

What if the story isn't "I'm not lovable"?

What if it's "I just haven't found people who speak my language yet"?

That version still holds the pain – but it also leaves room for hope.

And right now, that's all we need.

# Chapter 4:
# Surviving Loneliness
*(How to get through the hard days without falling apart.)*

Some days, loneliness is just a dull background hum.

Other days, it's a wave that hits you out of nowhere – when you wake up, when you walk past a group laughing, when you go to bed and realize no one texted all day.

You can know it's "normal."

You can know it "won't last forever."

And still feel like it might crush you today.

This chapter isn't about fixing it.

This is about surviving it.

Living through the quiet moments without letting them rewrite your worth.

## 🧘 Survival Rule #1:
## You don't have to earn rest or joy.

Loneliness often comes with shame.

You feel like you shouldn't enjoy things – like if you're this alone, maybe you don't deserve comfort.

So you skip the things that used to bring you peace:

The music, the art, the walks, the weird movies, the dumb video games.

But here's the thing: you *need* those things more than ever right now.

Pleasure, distraction, and comfort aren't luxuries – they're lifelines.

Joy isn't something you earn by being productive or socially successful.

Joy is something you're allowed to have *because you're human.*

## ✏ Try This: The Tiny Anchor List

Write down five things that feel comforting – even a little bit.

Not things that fix the problem. Just things that keep your head above water.

Some examples:

- Rewatching a show you've seen a hundred times
- Making a hot drink, even if you don't finish it
- Sitting outside, even if you're just on the steps
- Playing music with no lyrics, just sound
- Doing something with your hands: a puzzle, a doodle, a fidget toy

Now pick *one* to do today. Even for five minutes. That's it. No gold star needed.

## 📱 Survival Rule #2:
## Get offline (just a little)

The internet lies.

It shows people at their loudest, happiest, shiniest moments – filtered and cropped to look like "everyone else is doing fine."

But if you're already feeling disconnected, seeing that highlight reel will make you feel even worse.

You don't need to delete every app. Just give your brain breathing room.

Put your phone down while you eat.

Take a break from scrolling late at night.

Unfollow people who make you feel like you're falling behind.

Loneliness is hard enough without inviting curated perfection into your face all day.

## Survival Rule #3:
## Talk to someone – even if it's not the perfect person

When you feel invisible, it's easy to talk yourself out of reaching out.

You don't want to bother anyone. You think they'll be busy, annoyed, or fake-friendly.

So here's a shortcut:

Don't aim for a deep conversation.

Aim for *any* human connection.

Text someone a meme.

Comment on a YouTube video.

Ask the person at the checkout how their day's going.

Say hi to your dog like he's a roommate.

None of that fixes loneliness. But it reminds your brain that you *still exist in the world.*

That you're not entirely cut off. That you can still interact, still matter, still reach.

Even a tiny connection can give your system a reboot.

### 🗨 Survival Rule #4:
### Let it be today's problem, not forever's

Loneliness wants to trick you into thinking it's permanent.

You'll have one bad day, and your brain will whisper:

"See? This is just your life now."

But today's storm isn't tomorrow's forecast.

If you can remind yourself – *"This is how it feels right now, not how it will feel forever"* – you give yourself room to breathe.

Write that on a sticky note. Put it in your phone wallpaper. Say it out loud if you have to.

## ● Final Rule:
## Don't make big decisions from lonely logic

Loneliness can mess with your judgment.

You might:

• Chase after toxic friendships just to feel wanted

• Push people away to protect yourself

• Decide you'll "just be alone forever" and stop trying altogether

That's lonely logic talking. It's not the real you – it's survival mode.

Don't let the worst day make permanent decisions.

Wait until you've had a glass of water, gotten some sleep, or done one thing from your Anchor List.

Then reevaluate.

You're not behind. You're not failing.

You're surviving. And that's brave.

# Chapter 5:
# Reconnection Is Possible
*(You don't have to live like this forever – even if you've been stuck for a long time.)*

When you've felt lonely for a while, something strange starts to happen:

You get used to it.

Not because you like it.

Not because it's comfortable.

But because it becomes familiar.

You learn how to keep your guard up.

You learn how to keep expectations low.

You tell yourself, *"I'm better off this way,"* even if it aches.

And if that's where you are right now, I get it.

You survived something that should've broken you – and you did it by closing off. That's not weakness. That's instinct.

But here's the truth: even if loneliness became your normal...

**It doesn't have to stay your forever.**

## 🌱 **You might not even realize you're ready.**

Reconnection doesn't always start with a big, dramatic decision.

Sometimes, it starts with a small flicker of something:

- Curiosity when you overhear a conversation
- Feeling a little disappointed when a text *doesn't* come
- Wishing someone would ask how you're doing – and realizing you'd actually answer

That flicker? It matters. It means a part of you still *wants* connection.

Even if it's tiny. Even if you don't know what to do with it yet.

## 👣 Start small. Think soft steps, not giant leaps.

Reconnection doesn't mean diving headfirst into a group chat or hosting a party.

It can mean:

• Making eye contact and smiling at someone

• Leaving a supportive comment on someone's post

• Sending a funny video to a friend you've drifted from

• Asking a classmate if they want to study together

• Saying "hey" without overthinking what comes next

No expectations. No pressure. Just... a tiny reach.

Then maybe another.

Like touching the water before you decide to swim.

## 🔦 Reconnection isn't always with people first.

Sometimes the first bond you rebuild is with *yourself.*

That means:

- Letting yourself like weird things without shame
- Taking care of your space or your body like it deserves comfort
- Talking to yourself with kindness, not cruelty
- Saying "I matter" even when no one's around to confirm it

Because the better you treat yourself, the more likely you are to let others in.

You don't have to be fully healed to have relationships.

But reconnecting with yourself helps make those relationships healthier, more honest, and more real.

### 📄 **And when you're ready — flip the book.**

On the other side of this book is the next step.

Not in a "go out and change everything" kind of way.

But in a "now that I know what I need, maybe I'm ready to learn how to get it" kind of way.

You've survived something heavy.

You've looked your own loneliness in the eye and stayed.

That's not weakness. That's strength most people never talk about.

If even a small part of you wants to try again — wants to be seen, heard, understood...

Turn the book over.

I'll be there.

# Conclusion

If you made it through these pages, you've already done something powerful.

You looked your own loneliness in the face – without turning away. That takes honesty. And guts. And heart.

You didn't rush to fix everything.

You didn't try to pretend it wasn't real.

You just gave it space. And that matters more than most people know.

Loneliness doesn't mean you're broken.

It doesn't mean you're unlikable, or weird, or behind.

It means you're human – and your need for connection is showing up loud enough to hear.

And now that you *have* heard it, you get to choose what comes next.

Maybe today's not the day to fix anything. That's okay.

Maybe just knowing it's not your fault is enough right now.


But if you ever feel ready to take even one small step forward...


...the other side of this book is waiting for you.


You don't have to be fully healed to begin.

You just have to be willing to reach out – one imperfect, beautiful moment at a time.

Sometimes, loneliness isn't about being alone – it's about feeling invisible.

This side of the book is here for the quiet ache no one talks about. The feeling that you're left out of something everyone else seems to have.

It won't give you fake optimism or push you to "just get out there."

Instead, it will help you understand your own heart, soothe the sharp edges, and remind you that needing people doesn't make you weak – it makes you human.

Whether you're surrounded by others or sitting by yourself, you deserve to feel connected again.

Start here. Feel less alone.

www.ingramcontent.com/pod-product-compliance
Lightning Source LLC
Chambersburg PA
CBHW070124030426
42335CB00016B/2256

## Can't I Just

# Be a Good Friend?

Jennifer Larsen

# Contents

# Introduction

**You're not bad at friendship. You probably just never got the manual.**

Some people seem to come out of the womb knowing how to bond with others. They laugh at the right time, say the right things, make everyone feel like they belong.

If that's not you?

Welcome. You're in the right place.

This book isn't here to turn you into someone fake or hyper-social.

You don't need to be the life of the party to be a good friend.

You don't even need a ton of friends.

You just need *enough real connection* to feel grounded, seen, and wanted.

And here's the secret: **friendship isn't magic — it's a skill.**

One you can learn, practice, and get better at.

This side of the book will walk you through it.

We'll talk about:

- How to show warmth (even when you feel awkward)

- What makes people want to open up

- How to build closeness over time

- And how to stop accidentally pushing people away

None of this is about pretending.

It's about learning how to express what's already in you – and how to build something solid with the people who can actually meet you there.

Let's get into it.

## Chapter 1:
## People Can't Read Your Mind
*(And most of them are too busy wondering what you think of them.)*

Let's get this out of the way:

Most people aren't avoiding you because they don't like you.

They're just busy thinking about *themselves.*

They're wondering if you think they're cool, or awkward, or annoying.

They're worried about how they look, what they said earlier, whether they sounded stupid.

They're not rejecting you – they're just distracted by their own anxiety.

So what does that mean for you?

It means you can't wait for people to *magically notice* that you're friendly, kind, loyal, funny, or worth knowing.

You have to show it – just a little – so they have something to respond to.

## Friendship starts with signals.

If you want connection, you have to send *invitations.*

Not formal ones. Just signals. Tiny cues that say:

"I'm open. I'm safe. I'd like to talk."

Without those signals, people assume you want to be left alone.

Some ways to invite connection:
- **Look up** when someone enters the room
- **Make a little eye contact** – even for a second
- **Smile slightly** or nod
- **Say something small** like "Hey," "That's cool," or "Did you see what happened in class?"

These are like social green lights.

They don't guarantee anything – but they show people you're not a red light.

## 🗿 "But shouldn't they just get me?"

Honestly? No.

People can't see how interesting you are if you never speak.

They can't know you care if you never ask how they're doing.

They can't see your warmth if you stay completely silent, arms crossed, avoiding eye contact, waiting for someone to "get you."

That doesn't mean you're doing anything wrong.

But it means if you *want* connection, you have to be visible – just enough for someone to know where to start.

You don't have to be loud.

You don't have to tell your life story.

You just have to give people a reason to believe it's okay to talk to you.

## 🛠️ Try This:

For one day, experiment with sending *one* small signal of openness to someone you normally wouldn't talk to.

Examples:

- Say "Hey" to someone at your lunch table
- Hold the door and smile (just slightly)
- Compliment someone's hoodie
- Ask "Did you understand what that assignment was about?"

Then... stop. That's enough.

You're not trying to make a friend in one shot. You're just sending out little radio signals.

If someone tunes in, great. If not, that doesn't mean you failed.

It means you tried – and next time, it might land somewhere better.

## Chapter 2:
## How to Invite Connection
*(And why you're not the only one who needs it.)*

Let's get something straight right now:

**You're not the only one who wants to be seen.**

It might *feel* like that sometimes – like everyone else already has their group, their routine, their people.

Like you're the extra character wandering through other people's lives, hoping someone will toss you a line.

But here's the secret:

**Even the confident ones want to be noticed.**

Even the loud ones want to be heard.

Even the ones who walk with their arms around someone else's shoulders still wonder, deep down, if they truly belong.

## 🧠 Connection is not charity.

It's easy to fall into the mindset that connection is something other people *give* you – if you're interesting enough, charming enough, or lucky enough.

But that's not how this works.

Connection is *shared.*

And when you show up – even a little – you're not begging. You're offering.

You're saying:

"Hey, I see you. I'm here, too. Let's not be strangers."

That's not weakness. That's generosity.

## ● Tiny moments matter.

You don't have to pour your heart out to build connection.

Sometimes it's:

- A nod to the guy who holds the door

- A smile at the kid in the cafeteria who always sits alone

- A quiet "me too" when someone complains about the weather

- Holding eye contact half a second longer than usual

Those moments might feel small to you, but they could be everything to someone else.

Connection doesn't always start loud.

Sometimes it starts in a look, a pause, a breath.

## ● **People don't always show they're lonely.**

That person who looks like they have it all together?

Might not feel close to anyone.

The class clown? Might feel like no one takes them seriously.

The loud group in the hallway? Might just be going through the motions.

Even your teachers, your parents, your neighbor across the street –
**everybody is carrying something.**

You're not broken for needing connection.

You're human for noticing when it's missing.

And when you reach out, you're not just helping yourself – you might
be giving someone else the exact thing they were afraid to ask for.

## 🛠 How to Create Space for Connection:

You don't have to chase people. Just create a little opening.

Here's what that can look like:

## 🎤 Ask a small, low-stakes question:

"You see the test schedule yet?"

"What are you listening to?"

"Did that homework make any sense to you?"

People often need a reason to talk that doesn't feel too personal.

You're not being fake – you're just opening the door.

### 🖊 Actually listen — and give them space to talk about what they care about.

Let them share something they like, even if it's not your thing.

People bond more over being heard than being agreed with.

You can say:

"I don't know a lot about that, but that's cool."

"You sound like you're really into it."

"Tell me more?"

That's it. That's connection.

You don't need the perfect reply. You just need to care enough to stay present.

## 🌐 You are not a guest in other people's world.

You're not lucky just to be tolerated.

You belong here, same as everyone else.

You have value just by showing up.

And the truth is: **someone out there is hoping you notice them.**

So when you speak? You're not intruding.

When you look up? You're not being weird.

When you care? You're not being needy.

You're offering something that *everyone needs,* even if they're too guarded to say it.

Connection is mutual.

And you have every right to take your place in it.

## ⬤ Chapter 3: How to Seem Warm (Even If You Feel Awkward)

*(Because people don't always know you're kind unless you show it.)*

Here's a frustrating truth:

You can be the kindest, most loyal, most thoughtful person in the room –

and if your body language says "stay away,"

people will believe *that* before they believe what's true.

It's not fair. But it's real.

Most people decide whether or not you're "friendly" within a few seconds – long before they hear your best story or realize how great you are.

But that doesn't mean you have to become someone else.

It just means you need to understand how people *read you* – so you can make sure what you *feel* on the inside actually shows on the outside.

## 😐 The "Unintentionally Unapproachable" Problem

You might feel:

- Calm
- Tired
- Anxious
- Focused
- Unsure

But other people might see:

- Bored
- Uninterested
- Cold
- Judgy
- Mad

The disconnect between what you *feel* and what others *see* is huge – and often no one tells you it's happening.

So let's fix that.

### 💬 First: You Don't Have to Fake It

This isn't about acting fake or smiling nonstop.

You don't need to perform friendliness like a sales pitch.

But you do need to **signal that you're safe to talk to** – especially if you want someone else to feel brave enough to approach you.

Think of it like this:

If your body language is a closed door, people won't knock.

So we're just going to crack the door open.

## ☝ Quick Fixes That Change How You're Read:

### ◉ Eye Contact

You don't have to stare – but **glance up occasionally.**

Make short, gentle eye contact when someone's talking. Look away naturally.

Even two seconds makes a huge difference.

### ☺ Micro-Expressions

You don't need to beam. But let your **face react** to things.

Raise your eyebrows when someone says something surprising.

Let your mouth turn up just a little when someone's joking.

Signal that you're listening, not just waiting for them to stop talking.

26

## 🗨 Open Posture

Crossed arms, hunched shoulders, and earbuds scream "do not disturb."

Try sitting with your arms relaxed or hands visible.

Angle your body slightly toward the people around you, not away.

Even shifting your position can make you seem more welcoming.


## ▦ Put Your Phone Down

Phones are social shields. They say "I'm busy" even when you're just doom-scrolling.

If you want to seem open, give the room some of your attention.

You don't have to make a big deal of it – just *don't bury your face in the screen the whole time.*

### Why This Works (Even If It Feels Weird at First)

People aren't mind readers. They're cue readers.

When your face, body, or tone *seems* cold – even if you're not – others take that as a signal that you're not interested.

So when you adjust those signals *just slightly,* you're not becoming fake.

You're just making your warmth *visible.*

You're showing:

"Hey, I'm safe to talk to."

"I care what you're saying."

"I'm paying attention."

"You matter here."

That's not manipulation. That's communication.

## 🛠 Try This: The "Friendly Scan"

Pick one setting: a classroom, a group chat, the lunch table.

For just five minutes, try:

- Looking up once or twice
- Smiling gently when someone says something funny
- Nodding when someone talks
- Sitting in a way that faces the group (even slightly)

Then just watch what happens.

People may start to include you more – even if no words are exchanged.

That's the power of warmth made visible.

## Final Thought: You're Already Enough

You don't have to be the loudest.

You don't have to tell jokes.

You don't have to fake energy you don't have.

You just need to *let people see who you really are.*

Because the real you? The one who cares, who notices things, who wants connection?

They're worth seeing.

# 🤝 Chapter 4:
# Building Trust Over Time

*(Because real connection isn't instant – it's earned.)*

Let's clear something up:

Friendship isn't about saying the right thing once.

It's about showing up again and again, in small ways, until the other person starts to believe you mean it.

The people you're trying to get close to? They have their own walls, just like you.

They're nervous about being judged, rejected, forgotten, or misunderstood.

That means closeness doesn't happen because you had a "deep talk."

It happens when you show, consistently, that you're safe to be around.

## Trust Is Built in Small, Boring Moments

You don't need a trauma bond or some intense emotional reveal to earn trust.

You just need to:

- Say you'll show up – and then show up

- Remember something they told you

- Text when you said you would

- Keep your word on the little stuff

- Ask how they're doing *even when you don't need anything from them*

It's not flashy. But over time, it makes people feel safe around you.

And safety? That's where trust grows.

## ⬭ **Want to bond? Do something reliable.**

Consistency is one of the most underrated friendship tools ever.

People don't bond with the most exciting person.

They bond with the one who makes them feel secure.

That might be:

- The person who always saves them a seat
- The person who remembers they hate group work
- The person who checks in after a hard test
- The person who brings a snack to share every Friday

None of those things require deep conversation.

But they all say: *"I see you. You matter. I want to make space for you."*

### 🗨️ A Trick from Ben Franklin (Yes, Really)

Ben Franklin once wrote that a great way to build connection was to ask someone for a small favor – and then be gracious when they help you.

Why?

Because doing a favor makes people feel useful and valued.

It creates a little investment. A little bond.

Try:

- "Hey, can you remind me what that assignment was?"
- "Mind if I sit here?"
- "You seem good at this – can I ask you a quick question?"

Then say thank you.

Smile. Mean it. That's the glue.

You don't have to *impress* people to bond with them.

Sometimes letting someone *help you* is the connection.

## 😐 Vulnerability — But Only a Little at a Time

Here's where people mess up:

They either never open up at all, or they trauma-dump on someone who hasn't earned it yet.

Real friendship grows in layers.

Start small:

- "Today sucked."
- "That made me kind of nervous."
- "I'm not great at this, honestly."

These are invitations for someone to say, *"Same."*
That's where closeness begins.

You're not asking for pity — you're just being real.
And realness is magnetic.

## 🗨 Quick Tip: You Don't Need "Deep Talks" Every Time

Don't pressure yourself to make every hangout intense.

Friendship doesn't mean emotional marathons.

In fact, a lot of the strongest bonds are built in:

- Shared silence

- Inside jokes

- Repeating small routines

- Being around each other without having to perform

Let people be near you without needing to be *on.*

That's what real connection feels like.

**Final Thought: Don't Rush It**

If someone doesn't open up right away, it doesn't mean they don't like you.

They might need more time. More consistency. More signals that you're safe.

And if someone pulls away? That's not always a failure.

It just means they weren't the right one to invest in deeply – and that's okay.

You don't need hundreds of friends.

You just need a few *honest, safe ones.*

And you build those not with magic, but with time, care, and little signs that you're someone worth trusting.

And you are.

# Chapter 5:
# How to Go Deeper

*(When you're ready to move from "people I talk to" to "people I trust.")*

Surface-level friendship is easy to come by.

You say hey. You sit near each other. You share jokes or complain about the same things.

But real friendship – the kind where you feel seen, where you can relax, where you know someone's got your back – that takes something more.

You can't force it.

But you *can* recognize when it's possible... and gently help it grow.

**☘ First Sign: You're not performing anymore.**

You've stopped trying to impress them.

You don't need to filter every word.

You feel like you can show up tired, or quiet, or weird – and they don't make you feel bad about it.

That's the beginning of safety. And safety is the beginning of closeness.

### 🧠 Second Sign: They make space for you, too.

If someone:

- Checks in when you're off
- Listens when you talk
- Remembers things you said last week
- Doesn't dominate every interaction

...that's someone who's not just there to be heard. They want to *hear you,* too.

You don't have to earn their attention. It's already being offered.

That's a green flag.

## How to Deepen the Bond (Without Getting Weird)

Once you sense the door is open, you can step through it gently.
Here's how:

### 1. Appreciate out loud.

Say the thing most people just think.

"I'm really glad we've been hanging out."
"You're easy to talk to."
"Thanks for always being chill about stuff."
"You're good at making people feel comfortable."

You'd be amazed how powerful this is – especially when said casually.
It's not emotional oversharing. It's just honesty.

And most people *never* hear this stuff... even though they crave it.

## 2. Ask something slightly deeper.

When the vibe feels right, try:

"What's something you wish more people understood about you?"

"Is that something you've always liked, or did you get into it recently?"

"What's something that helps when you're stressed?"

Questions like that show curiosity – and give them permission to go deeper, too.

You're not prying. You're inviting.

## 3. Let them help you sometimes.

Even just saying, "Can I run something by you?" or "I feel weird about something – can I vent for a sec?"

Letting someone support you creates trust.

And when you receive help well – by being appreciative, not dramatic – it strengthens the bond without dumping weight on them.

## ♡ **What if they don't respond?**

Not everyone's ready.

Not everyone knows how to connect.

If someone shuts down, gets awkward, or disappears when you try to go deeper – it doesn't mean you messed up.

It just means that person wasn't your person. Not right now.

That doesn't cancel all your progress.

It just means you keep going. Keep building. Keep showing up for yourself and the people who *do* respond.

## ⬭ One Last Thing:

Sometimes you'll try to go deeper with someone, and they just... won't go with you.

Not because you did something wrong. But because they:

- Don't have the emotional tools
- Don't know how to connect that way
- Aren't in a place where they can give more than surface-level friendship

And that's okay.

It doesn't mean the connection was fake. It doesn't mean you failed.

Some people will stay acquaintances. Some will drift.

Some will appreciate you but never show it clearly.

And some will only know how to take, not give.

You're allowed to keep being kind without giving your whole self away.

You can offer connection *without committing all your energy* to someone who doesn't feel safe or balanced to be around.


Being a good friend doesn't mean overextending.

It means caring where it's safe to care – and being wise enough to know the difference.


You deserve connection that lifts you up.

And if someone isn't there yet? Let them walk their own path. You've got yours.

# Conclusion

If you've made it this far, it means something inside you wants real connection – not just company, but *honest belonging.*

That's brave. And rare.

You're not just learning how to "make friends."

You're learning how to be someone who *builds trust, shows care, and gives people room to feel safe.*

That's a gift to the world.

Not everyone will respond.

Not every moment will go the way you hoped.

But every step you've taken toward kindness, courage, and connection – that stays with you.

Even trying matters.

So whether you've already made someone feel seen, or you're still waiting for someone to see you, know this:

You are becoming the kind of person someone will feel lucky to know.

And that makes all of this worth it.

Wherever you started – whether in loneliness or in learning to connect – you've made progress.


Maybe you don't feel wildly different. That's okay.

Change doesn't always feel loud. Sometimes it's quiet. Gentle. Invisible at first.


But it builds.


Every time you choose reflection over avoidance, kindness over fear, growth over self-blame – you change your direction.

And direction matters more than speed.


You don't have to "fix" everything at once.

You don't have to fake confidence or pretend things don't hurt.

You just have to *keep showing up* – for yourself, and when you're ready, for the people who'll meet you there.


This book might be done. But your story isn't.

There's more good ahead. And you're already on the way.

# 🤝 About Wayfinder Foundation Inc.

Wayfinder Foundation Inc. is a nonprofit dedicated to helping people build real-life skills, explore meaningful paths, and feel more capable in their day-to-day lives. We create accessible tools, books, and programs for students, parents, educators, and adults—because everyone deserves a roadmap and a little encouragement.

Learn more or support our book donation and outreach efforts at:

🔗 WayfinderFoundationInc.org

# 📑 Also by This Author

*Can't I Just Stop Feeling So Alone?* And *Can't I Just Be a Good Friend* are part of the *"Can't I Just...?"* Collection

Practical books for people figuring it out one day at a time:

- *Can't I Just Stay in My Room?* (Career guide for teens)

- *Can't I Just Skip College?* (Alternatives to traditional college)

- *Can't I Just Help My Kid Pick a Path?* (Parents' guide to careers for teens)

- *Can't I Just Be Like Everyone Else?* (Teen soft skills)

- *Can't I Just Hit Reset?* (Forgiveness for kids)

- *Can't I Just Start Over?* (Forgiveness for teens)

- *Can't I Just Do Something Fun?* (Teen hobbies)

- *Can't I Just Do Something for Me?* (Adult hobbies)

- *Can't I Just Get It Together?* (Adult soft skills)

- *Can't I Just Stop Feeling So Alone? /
  Can't I Just Be a Good Friend* ← you're here

- More on the way.

## 💼 About the Author

Jennifer Larsen writes books for people who are trying—trying to grow, trying to figure things out, trying not to lose it in the grocery store parking lot. She's the founder of Wayfinder Press and the Wayfinder Foundation, where she creates real-world tools that make life a little easier and a lot more human. She believes soft skills are survival skills, and everyone deserves support, no matter how late they're learning.

Wherever you started – whether in loneliness or in learning to connect – you've made progress.


Maybe you don't feel wildly different. That's okay.

Change doesn't always feel loud. Sometimes it's quiet. Gentle. Invisible at first.


But it builds.


Every time you choose reflection over avoidance, kindness over fear, growth over self-blame – you change your direction.

And direction matters more than speed.


You don't have to "fix" everything at once.

You don't have to fake confidence or pretend things don't hurt.

You just have to *keep showing up* – for yourself, and when you're ready, for the people who'll meet you there.


This book might be done. But your story isn't.

There's more good ahead. And you're already on the way.